Sweetie

How much should you give up
to keep that relationship?
I can answer that!

Debra J. Palardy

Sweetie

Produced and printed by Stillwater River Publications.

Visit our website at
www.StillwaterPress.com
for more information.

First Stillwater River Publications Edition

ISBN: 978-1-955123-59-4

Library of Congress Control Number: 2021921967

12345678910
Written by Debra J. Palardy
Cover Design by Lindsay Whelan
Published by Stillwater River Publications,
Pawtucket, RI, USA.

Publisher's Cataloging-In-Publication Data
(Prepared by The Donohue Group, Inc.)

Names: Palardy, Debra J., author.
Title: Sweetie : how much should you give up
to keep that relationship? I can answer that! / Debra J. Palardy
Description: First Stillwater River Publications edition.
Pawtucket, RI, USA : Stillwater River Publications, [2021]
Previously published in 2016.
Identifiers: ISBN 9781955123594
Subjects: LCSH: Dating violence | Dating (Social customs)
Teenagers—Sexual behavior | Interpersonal relations
LCGFT: Self-help publications
Classification: LCC HQ801.83 .P35 2021 |
DDC 306.73--dc23

The best things in life are free;
unless you're a victim
of domestic violence!

Foreword

There's a reason that *Sweetie* came to be. I wanted to protect my children from the horror that they could be subjected to someday, and I now knew just how to prevent it.

Even though I like to consider myself an intelligent person, many years ago I found myself trapped in a violent relationship.

As you read *Sweetie,* you'll see that there are many reasons why women get trapped in these relationships. Not one of them is because of their intelligence. *Sweetie* has all the real-life experiences or warning signs that would have helped me if I had known them ahead of time. I knew the fact that my children were intelligent wasn't going to keep them from being at risk.

Every person has the same vision of their true love. They imagine a person who sees them, really sees them for what they are. They imagine a person who hangs on their every word and thinks only of them all day. They imagine a person who spends all their time making them feel like there is no one else in the world for them. They imagine a person who spends every minute away at work or running daily errands longing to be reunited.

That's what abusers have as their disguise. It has awesome power and capabilities. So it's easy to see why so many get intelligent people caught up in it. I knew my children would have this image of their true love. We have all the same image. I knew they might be at risk someday.

Domestic violence crosses every tax bracket. It can be found on every corner of the planet, from the most poverty-stricken, to the most affluent. Many victims of domestic violence do have enough of their own money to get out and pay their own way, yet they don't get out.

I knew having educated, self-sufficient children wouldn't keep them from being at risk. I knew that once they read *Sweetie*, they would know what domestic violence looked like, felt like, sounded like, and even how to end it. In fact, they would also know the most important thing of all;

why if domestic violence came knocking at their door, they could not keep it.

We are all at risk, without education, on domestic violence coming at the right time. Since these abusers don't have the label **Abuser** tattooed on their foreheads, entering into a relationship with one is extremely easy. In other words, the abuser's fangs don't come out in the beginning of the relationship. So, the right time is before he thinks of you as his property, which meant they would have to learn it before they even met their abuser. Becoming a victim, and then doing damage control later, has proven time, and time again not to work.

One of our now infamous ex-presidents stated that domestic violence is one of the largest killers of adult women in the United States and should be fought as aggressively as any other life-threatening disease. I don't know the narrow definition of a disease, but I do know the broad one.

Getting a disease will adversely change your life, or end it, and everyone is susceptible. If there were a safe vaccine for domestic violence, my children would have gotten it. There wasn't, so I created one, and it's called *Sweetie*.

Sweetie

Alas, but there is just one problem!

He is always telling you that your friends are bad news. He says he can see it even if you can't. It's not just your friends. It's your family too. He complains about your clothes too, so you won't be embarrassed—or so he says. Sometimes he even asks who are you trying to impress. No matter how many times you tell him you dress for yourself he just doesn't seem to get it. He responds as though you are speaking another language. Let's get it out in the open; he loves you so much he is insanely jealous.

*There is not really a problem,
he just loves you that much.*

It wouldn't happen if he didn't love you so much, right? Isn't that what he says? Well guess what. If you're not his first you will find out he was this jealous before. It is not hard to find out. Does the thought of him being jealous with someone else strike a nerve?

It should. He tells you the intensity of your relationship is born from the way you make him feel.

He keeps telling you your problems are unique to the love the two of you share. He's lying. There is nothing unique about a control freak.

Believe me, he has had or will have the same problems with any relationship he will ever be in his whole life. You're just the current person having their spirit sucked dry by him.

There is jealousy, and then there is this!

He is not just jealous. *He is insanely jealous.* He doesn't want you to do the following things. This is just the short list. There is much more:

Talk to other guys.
Watch TV with other guys in it.
What does that leave?
Read magazines
Wear makeup
Wear pretty clothes
See your friends
Make phone calls
Go shopping without him,
even with your mother.
Work in a public place
Look out the passenger side window
of the car.
He ***"LOOKS"*** in your bag
Read novels
And much, much more.

Let's face it, anything and everything that does not put you right in his presence and under his complete control. He wants to isolate you from everyone. It's classic. Don't let him. If he gets **his** way you **will** lose yours—unless you're super human. Are you?

Have I gotten your attention yet?

Does any of this sound familiar? What about the violence that occurs when some of these things happen? They don't even have to be of your doing. They might be things that had to happen. For instance, you might have to go shopping with your mother. You can't disappoint her.

Does he question you as soon as he sees you? Does he want to know if you saw anyone you knew while you were out? If you tell him "No," does he believe you? If you did see someone you know, did you feel intense fear at the prospect of telling him?

You should! Does he call you a thousand times? Does he need to know who else might be calling you? If someone did call you, did you feel intense fear at the prospect of telling him? You should!

Did you realize that if you didn't tell him someone called, you are now keeping a secret from him? You are now in fact, a liar. That doesn't make you feel very good. Sure, it was his fault for being so scary about such petty things—or was it? You're the one allowing this relationship to continue. If you're in a relationship that turns you into a liar, you can only imagine how far down that dark road you might travel.

You can only imagine how many more things that were once unimaginable might suddenly seem acceptable. After a while you won't have to imagine—you'll know.

Do you realize that almost any inmate in any correctional institution across the country has way more freedom than you do right now? When you see him and none of the things you tell him seems to comfort him, does he have a familiar look in his eyes right before he strikes?

When I say *strike*, I mean verbally or physically. Abuse is abuse. Does he ask you to leave your home to make one with him? Does he ask this because he just hates to part at the end of the day? Trust me, that is not the reason. He needs you alone and under his control. Look out for that request. It's coming. There is nothing more predictable than a control freak looking for the ultimate control over you and all your stuff. One of their favorite things to do is threaten to ruin all your things if you don't obey. Trust me, it works like a charm. Nobody wants their lifelong collection of material objects and clothes to end up looking like it just went through a bear attack. It's the beginning of the end. Sometimes the end takes years off your life, literally.

Do not move in with this person! Whenever you say "No" to him in any way or upset him in the slightest there is an argument. If you're living with him there is nowhere to run while he is having one of his many tantrums. Also, you won't have the right to leave in the middle of one. You'll be trapped.

He said he was sorry!

This is when the crying starts. He has no problem crying if it will fix the mess he made. Mostly it is you crying. I'd rather not go into the details of being insulted, accused, and hit by him. Let me just say this—when he does leave a mark on your body he'll make you tell the people who are **still** in your life, the ones he hasn't been able to eliminate yet, that you hurt yourself in some other way. You'll be telling them you hit yourself on a door or something. You'll be hurting yourself when you obey this absurd request because you'll be lying **again.** This time you'll be lying to people you've most likely **never** lied to. When in an abusive relationship you will spend a lot of time lying to everyone—you'll have to. If you don't lie to him he'll get angry. If you don't lie to the people who love you they'll be onto what is going on with you and him; then they will have to start to help you get free. While you're still lying to them, you won't see the need to be set free yet. Of course, you won't see the fact that you are already burning the candle at both ends either. Still, you will be. There will be a clue; you'll be exhausted.

There are other people who will be hurt by the situation you're in as well; they are the people who **do** love you. As long as you have people who do love you, there is no such thing as only hurting yourself, there just isn't. I could go on for volumes on that topic. I won't. I need all of your attention right now just to get you to help yourself.

Circle of Pain

The situation that you're in could easily be called a Circle of Pain. I can elaborate. He will abuse and apologize, abuse and apologize. It's a vicious cycle or circle, if you will, with nothing but pain. The important thing is that he is sorry, right? He is so sorry. He couldn't be sorrier. That's when he becomes so sweet. He says all the right things. He tells you how stupid he is and repeats all the things you are thinking and hoping he should be saying.

How does he know what you're thinking? He tells you, in great detail, everything he did wrong and promises he will never let anything like that happen again. His eyes twinkle with softness and his arms feel so gentle. You melt at the sight of him saying all the right things. You know he really means it because your relationship is amazing and intense once again. These guys make up as hugely as they mess up. It's classic.

Yeah sure, he is like
hot and cold running water,
but when he's hot, he's HOT.

None of your friends have it so good! All of their boyfriends are interested in other things, not just their girlfriends. They spend time every day pursuing other interests beyond their relationships, and so do the girls.

Your boyfriend only wants to see you and nothing else. He's a true boyfriend—not like those other boys who think they can have a girlfriend and a life too. That's just how you'll feel—until it happens again. When it happens again you'll find yourself thinking that every last one of your friends has it better than you—even the ones without a boyfriend. You are bothered; but you just have to make him understand how much you love him. Once you do that, then there won't be any more of these troubles. You'll have it all. Right? Wrong!

How can that be wrong?

Your boyfriend is a violent, jealous, control freak. He is addicted to, and committed to, having complete control over you and your relationship. You won't be able to make your worlds work together to create a world that ***you*** can **thrive** in.

While his ego seems to be the problem, I will prove that we don't even know what the problem really is. In fact, not even professionals who have studied this situation for years really understand what causes this to happen. They will also admit that they don't know of a way to fix it. That's right, no cure. They claim they can help fifteen percent of those who come for help, and only slightly. Typically, no one seeks help unless they have been in jail more than once for hurting the people they claim to love. This time, that happens to be you. Do the math. That's eighty-five percent not helped at all.

In the meantime, I looked up *thrive* in the dictionary for you. Here is the meaning of that word. It sometimes helps me to hear it out loud. It means to develop vigorously and flourish. It also means to be successful.

When you are in a relationship with a person who is not helping you grow as a person you cannot thrive. What's worse, the woman you should grow into can never be.

In other words, if you are not free to explore you, then you can never grow to become whoever that might be. You **cannot** thrive in this relationship. I don't mean until you two get it right; I mean you will **never** thrive in this relationship. Simply put, you **won't** be thriving! You will suffer a lot more harm than not growing as a person as well. I can support that claim.

Maybe other women can't, but you can!

You're not hearing me yet. I know why. The reason is you have these feelings of love that are real. They are as real as his mood swings. You know those are real. They have threatened you enough times. Where your feelings for him are coming from you don't know. You do know, however, that they are real. Your love for him will prevail. It is strong enough to mold him and shape him. It is strong enough to get him to a level of conscientiousness he has never known.

Once you're through with him, this scared, insecure man won't exist. The only thing that will exist is this amazing man and the bond between the two of you that can never be broken. Not only that, he will know that he has you to thank for helping him become that man.

That will be a shining day in your life, and you spend lots of time thinking about it. It always brings a smile to your face and a glow in your heart. You can't wait for that day to come. You're going to be waiting for that day forever. I can support that claim.

Let's first find out
where these feelings
you are having are coming from,
and where they might lead.

Yes, those strong feelings can't be false. They are real all right. Do you know what they are? They are the ones you will be using to be a mom. Yes that's right—a mom. It's called the maternal instinct. Remember—shape, mold, love into the final product. The problem is, he has already been raised. He's done. ***He is the final product***. He is not going to change, EVER.

If you need to explore those feelings, have a baby someday. Would you like to hear something scary? If you have his baby, you will spend countless hours telling him that you love him as much as the baby. Confused? I can clear that up. He will actually be jealous of his own baby too! Only that's the good news. The bad news is that you might be instead trying to convince him that it ***was*** his baby.

It could also be an object. Yes, he can be jealous of an object too; it only has to take you away from giving him all of your attention. Sound stupid? It is just the tip of the iceberg of stupidity in this type of situation.

If you are having his baby, whatever you do, don't ever take it out on the baby. It will only hurt you and the baby, forever. I realize that being young, you have probably never experienced anything with so many highs and lows. Again, these guys make up as hugely as they mess up.

The adrenaline and/or endorphins you get struggling in this relationship are the things that you will really miss, not him. You could be hooked on chemicals that your own body makes, and he sets them off. I can't think of too many things that will age you faster than being a Circle of Pain adrenaline and/or endorphin junkie. That may be a term I made up, but it is to explain a very real problem. Later, I will elaborate further on how to better identify this Circle, which will help you to break it. In the meantime, why don't you just park yourself on a giant piece of foil in the blazing sun, skip the sunscreen, and get it over with? In other words, it gets old and so will you; fast. Your goose will be cooked.

You will wait forever.
I can support that claim.

The expression that "girls mature faster" is as old as the hills. That's because it's true. You know this to be true on some level but you've probably always thought that there was some cut-off point. What I mean is, at some point when you both became adults, it levels off and you both mature at the same rate. This is not true. It happens forever. Women are a constant work in progress. It feels like you are always changing your hair, clothes, and style, but it is much deeper than that. It's internal too, and it never stops working at a faster rate than the male population.

All men seem to mature at the same speed—slow. They don't, however, start out at the same degree of maturity or wellness, if you will. That's why when picking a partner you have to get a good one from the start.

Even if you do get a good partner there will still be several years, for us women, of waiting for him to catch up; for lack of a better expression. That's the good news. When you get a good one from the start it will all eventually come to fruition. Some women claim it's right around the time they retire and live out the rest of their years free of work and financial woes. The man they married finally becomes the man of their dreams.

The bad news is, all men mature at the same slow rate. So if you start out with a guy with huge problems, especially a jealous control freak, by the time he finally becomes a normal man he will be over three hundred years old. You don't have that kind of time.

You will wait forever, plus two hundred years. There are murderers in prison who got less of a sentence than that. For clarity, that is a long time—after giving him the best years of your life and you've lost all your friends, your family, your career, your dreams, and your **girlish figure**! It's also after you've raised your sons to become women abusers and your daughters to think this is the normal way women live. Your children don't have that kind of time either.

Have a little faith!

Have you ever wondered why he doesn't trust you? You've probably never given him any reason not to. He has you believing that it will just kill him if he ever lost you. He tells you that's the reason he just can't take any chances that you might stray. This makes you feel all warm and glowing inside. Well, it should leave you cold! Here's why.

There is a good reason why you won't take everything away from him just to keep him. It's because you have faith. I looked up *faith* for you in my beloved dictionary. It means confidence or trust in a person. It also means having loyalty and fidelity without first having proof. There will never, ever be enough proof for a person without any faith. Ask yourself—do you want to lose someone who is close to you? Of course you don't. No one does. But you go through your life having faith. You have faith in yourself and in others. That takes inner strength. This inner strength is something that you either have or you don't have. It's something you have to get growing up. If he doesn't have it, he doesn't have it. Your faith needs an equal. In other words, the best you can do for you is find someone who not only has faith, but also will put their faith in you and hope to get yours in return.

Does that sound like your present situation? You don't have to say it out loud. You only have to hear it said inside. Once the question has been asked you can't stop the answer from coming.

He is the one with the problem, not you.

Did you ever make the mistake of asking him why he doesn't trust you? If you have, then you've heard him say, "It's not you I don't trust; it's it all those jerks out there I don't trust." That's priceless! What does he expect you to do with that information? Does he expect you to wait for the world to change before you go to the store? There are plenty of people who are not worth trusting. **So what?** Every one of us on this planet involved in a committed relationship has no choice but to allow their partners to move about freely amongst the untrustworthy.

The only ones they have to trust are their partners. Your boyfriend doesn't trust **you** because he doesn't know how and never will. That is a huge problem. He is a type with a title, he's textbook. I looked up *trust* for you. Here is what it means—it's when someone puts their faith in another's integrity. He's not doing that on any level.

I'm sure you have plenty of integrity. I'm sure others in your life can see it and put their faith in it repeatedly. You will never enjoy that pleasure from him. I might point out that it's a right, not a privilege, to enjoy that pleasure from your partner. You will need to do some research on battered women. I strongly suggest you actually speak to a few of those shattered women.

You will find the biggest mystery is—why do they stay? It's those mom feelings. They are intense, but they are meant for your children.

They are not meant for your mate, EVER. In fact, using your mom instincts with your mate is plain creepy. Those feelings are a very powerful tool. With any powerful tool used incorrectly you could get hurt. You are absolutely using it incorrectly. I have heard countless times, "There is no greater power than that of a mother's love." If you're thinking of waiting until these feelings die down, here is a hint—your maternal instincts are forever and when challenged get more powerful.

His distrust and constant needs are a challenge to your maternal instincts. Your maternal instincts scream when your children are floundering in any way that you need to hang in and hang on to your relationship with them until the crisis passes. Remember that powerful tool? You're **not** his mother!

I can't explain why these instincts are getting mixed up. I can, however, give you an example of how our natural instincts don't always serve us. Are you, or anybody you know, terrified of the dentist? Well if you really think about it, the pain, if any, is not that bad. Yet, we sweat and feel like we are driving ourselves to our own executions when we have to go. Some of us don't go.

Our instincts, in this case, are to protect our heads in a time of attack from predators. Our instincts are screaming that the dentist is a predator. They fabricate pure fear so we will listen to the command of not letting him get to our head. When our instincts are not serving us, like with our dentist and/or our mate that isn't allowing us to thrive, we need to use the backup plan, which is **our brain**. Identify the problem and then you have made incredible steps to solving it as well.

Is it just a lot of Hoopla?

I'd like to explore your maternal instincts just a bit more. I can identify what your maternal instincts feel like in this situation. They don't feel like you are trying to raise him. They feel like your love can make him well. It can't. It's bigger than you. His problem is so deep that it's a part of him like his hair and eye color. Do you think you could love him so much that his hair and eyes would change colors? You know you can't. Even the counselors who treat these men for this type of problem claim that eighty-five percent of the time they don't get helped at all. The fifteen percent that do are not perfect either. Those are your odds. That's what I meant by misusing the powerful tool of your maternal instincts. In this case, you will get hurt. Meanwhile, your girlfriends with their relationships that seemed cool and reserved are not using their maternal instincts to keep their boyfriends. They are using the instincts needed to have a partner.

Having known women in both of these kinds of relationships, I can assure you that normal relationships are anything but cool and reserved. The people who don't feel the need to show everyone how much they love each other in public on a regular basis are definitely hiding something. They are hiding how amazing their relationship is. To say *hiding* wouldn't really be accurate. What they are doing is just between them, and they are both fine leaving it that way.

So to you it seems cool and reserved. But if you were ever in a normal relationship, you would know there was nothing cool or reserved about a normal relationship. It was just private, as it should be. I can't tell you how many famous people, and some not famous people, I have heard rave about their fabulous relationships. They are always the ones who seem to go down in flames later on. Meanwhile the other people who just sit by and don't feel the need to announce it to everyone in earshot have relationships that go on and on.

You have to wonder, who are these people are trying to convince? Us, or themselves? I wouldn't be afraid to land in a quiet, normal, and seemingly reserved relationship. You might not be trying to purposely demonstrate how great your relationship is, but it's still happening. He's doing that. So who is he doing it for?

My personal theory on relationships.

I have this theory on relationships and marriage. Here it is—everyone in a relationship or a marriage is with some sort of a quirky jerk, absolutely everyone. I can't tell you how many friends came crying on my shoulder about not being able to find a great guy. I have always told them the same thing. Look for a jerk. I love the funny, confused look on their faces. "That's what I said; look for a jerk."

What I actually mean is; compile a list of the

little things that bother you or that you would hate about a guy, and look for a guy that has the shortest and most benign things on that list. They should be things that he will do while you are in a bad mood and things he will do while you are in a horrible mood too.

After you have done that, all the good stuff should already be in place. You need to be with the kind of quirky jerk you can tolerate. I say *tolerate* because that just what you will be doing. You won't be shaping, molding or fixing. You will be tolerating, tolerating, tolerating. When they say a relationship takes hard work, they are not talking about the passion. That's the easy part. Everyone can do that well. They are talking about the not-so-attractive things that you didn't or wouldn't notice at first. Everyone has them—I mean everyone.

You can't stay with anyone who has quirky jerky things that make you crazy. That's because when you later find yourself cemented into this relationship, they get bigger. They get so big that you can't see the guy you fell for in the first place. I would definitely consider someone who takes every last thing you enjoy away from you for his own personal pleasure, until death do you part, something I can't tolerate. Wouldn't you?

I am compelled to point out here something that most women would never tolerate—you will not be allowed to be in a bad mood. The only mood you will ever be allowed is trepidation. I looked up *mood* for you; it's a receptive state of mind predisposing to action. *Trepidation* is a fear about something that might happen.

Here is a list of the things
that don't make up a quirky jerk;
They're just things that make pure jerks.
You should avoid them at all costs
when looking for a partner.

Does he drive drunk?
This broad lack of concern for himself and everyone else could cost you your life.

Does he hate keeping a job?
This is a biggie. There isn't enough paper in the world to explain. Just trust me.

Does he have no visible goals for the future?
He might not be planning to have a future, and he's taking you with him.

Does he hate your pet?
If you love your pet he should respect that. The big concern is, who's next?

Does he have an addictive personality?
This isn't limited to the taking of substances. It's behavior too.

Does he openly hate people unlike him?
That's a huge clue! He'll eventually find out that you are not like him.

Does he exhibit road rage while you are in the car?
That's a big red flag.

Does he have an unhappy, complicated relationship with his parents or his mother?
You will be next.

Does he anger easily?
This is huge! Life is full of stress
that he can't deal with.

Does he think women are supposed to serve men and do what they are told?
This seems cute at first but gets old fast.

Does he make money but never has money?
This is a sign of something dark,
not related to money!

Does he spend countless hours complaining about everything
and nothing?
This seems benign at first, but if you're in a committed relationship it's a biggie.

Does he always seem to be
keeping a secret?
He is!

Is he insanely jealous and controlling?
This one will cost you everything you have; mind, body, spirit and maybe your life.

What could you be satisfied with?

If you can tolerate walking on eggshells and being jumpy and scared all the time then the two of you might really have something there. You must be prepared to wipe out any personal dreams you had for your future.

Remember, he doesn't want you to do anything or go anywhere. If you didn't plan to be healthy mentally and physically for the rest of your life, then you can keep him. If you have any kind of plans for your future, which might include anything from running to the store to pick up milk, to becoming the President of the United States, then you need to use those intense feelings to be the best mom in the world. Please don't use them on someone who is already raised.

What's the alternative?

If you stay with him, the saddest part is what you will lose. You will lose your true love, your freedom, and some women lose their lives. There are thousands of women in graves right now whose relationships started just like yours.

These women ended up in graves for several reasons. One of the biggest reasons is that they matured and got thoroughly sick of their lifestyles. They ended up making a stand. Not all of them end up in graves. Some of them wind up in prison; a real one with walls and guards

Right now, you're in a prison that he built for you. Some of them end up in counseling trying to come to grips with the fact that they took someone's life—their husband's.

The fact is, you will mature. You will get sick of living under his rock. Why wait until your life is ruined? By most people's standards it's already ruined. You prove that to yourself every time, deep in your heart, you wish that you could do something with your friends without his going off the deep end. That's a sure sign that you are already maturing and will mature even further. It is also a sign that your life is, to a point, already ruined. No one has to ask you to say it out loud.

You really are in serious trouble right now.

Unfortunately, you're the only one who can save you. **What about** what you're feeling? Your feelings are *real—they are.* You need to sit down and make a list of the feelings that you will need to be a girlfriend or a wife. Fear is not one of them. Some of them are trust, love, happiness, and living with and tolerating some faults that you won't be changing, molding or fixing. Again, love is one of them but is not always enough. You're full of love. Your ability to love is not the problem here. It's his ability to love that's the problem. Another problem is that he could live to be in his hundreds. Are you so scared to break up with him that you're just planning to wait for him to die of natural causes? That's a long time to spend with the wrong man. Remember the phrase "nobody's perfect." That phrase was made up by some smart ass who knew what he was and that he would always be what he was, just like everyone else would. That means your jealous boyfriend too. Of course, any good counselor will tell you that. In short, the right partner will be an ass from time to time too. Only there's a world of difference between being angry and hiding in a closet. What about your right to be an ass sometimes? It's gone!

Still want to keep this relationship?

Keeping this relationship could never be on the table for discussion. There can never be a foreseeable goal that you could strive for since not even he knows what it is. When I say goal, I mean specific rules you could follow which would guarantee not to make him upset again. The only thing he will know is that the two of you are not there yet, and that you are the reason. That is one thing that he will be sure of. I looked up the word *rule*. Here it is: It is a regulation governing your conduct. It also means exercising dominant power. Ah, Love! Even if he did have a list of rules you would have to memorize them and implement them in each different situation that the two of you found yourselves in on a daily basis. No problem, right? That will be one of your biggest problems. Frustrated yet? If you are, that's the good news. That means you're hearing me now. There's more good news as well. You're a wonderful person. Without him, you will eventually be all right. With him...?

What is really at stake here?

You could be with your life partner for decades and decades. You will not be changing him. You will be tolerating him as is. This means your mate has to be the kind of quirky jerk that doesn't suck the life out of you.

People do mature with age. His type doesn't mature in the same way. They sometimes get worse as they get older. Some experts will tell you they always get worse. So you know, they do always get worse.

Pay close attention to the news. You will be amazed when you hear reports of domestic violence and how long these women have been going through it—that is, if you're still allowed to watch the news.

I'm sure those women thought that their guys would mature too. They didn't. By the time it makes the news, these girlfriends are wives. Right now you're a girlfriend. Get out while the getting is good! Later, it **will** take super human strength. Do you possess super human strength? Breaking up is hard. It is the death of a dream. Every girl or woman who lets a person into her heart has planned her whole future looking into his eyes. That's hard to let go of. I understand that. Remember, your instincts don't always serve you. You might need to switch to "Plan B" in your brain. If you do, your brain will tell you that you had plans for your future **before him** that could come true, and the beautiful plans you have **with him** never will. Your instincts are not serving you. Another problem is being a woman. When we feel like we are in love, we make a space for our partner in our hearts shaped just like him. No one else can fill that shape but the person we let in. Let your heart soften by imagining the future with your dreams in it. Do it a lot. Treat it like an exercise; it is. Soon you will see you can only have your dreams and a partner as long as it's not him.

You need to understand—staying with him is going suck all the good stuff from your soul. Your true partner has eyes you can look into forever while dreaming things that can actually happen. If you break up it won't be the death of a dream. It will be the death of a nightmare instead. Nightmares need to end. He is the wrong guy, but that doesn't make ending a relationship any easier. You will live. I promise you. It may be the only reason you do live. After you make the break, the first thing you will get back is that inner voice that says, "Hey, You. Let's go here, watch this, and wear that." Do you remember her? Remember how much fun she was? That inner voice is one of the most wonderful things about you. You will have the rest of your life to explore that voice. After all, that inner voice is what makes you *you*. It's what he should love about you. Wondering what you could possibly do next should be the **most exciting thing** to your true love. It is not something he would ever, ever stomp out. Take a look at the big picture—your community will be robbed of the contributions you are meant to make.

Is he as isolated as you are?

Please don't make the mistake of thinking he is experiencing the same isolated life that you are having; he is not.

There are several ways he will pull this off. One of them is he will make sure that you're safely tucked into whatever spot it is that he is happiest with—and then start a fight.

As you know, when he decides that the two of you are going to fight, then that is just what you will do. When the fight is where he wants it to be he will leave. When you see him next, one of two things will happen. You will either not ask him where he went, or you will make the mistake of asking. You will, naturally, not want to start an argument. He's counting on it. If you don't ask him, you probably won't find out. If you ask, you'll open a can of worms that nobody wants opened. If you decide to make a stand and ask, he will turn it around on you and ask you questions. "Did anybody call or come over?"

No matter what you tell him he won't believe you. By the time your life is over, you will have accumulated as much time answering the same stupid questions over and over, as some people accumulate enjoying themselves. If you do the math, you will be amazed at how much time that is cut out of the enjoyment part of your life. This kind of thing will repeat itself again and again. It has to, because he wants to do things with other people. We all do. Does that sound fair? Does it sound familiar?

It sounds sad doesn't it? It should. It is! You're letting a bully take your whole life instead of just your lunch money.

Why are you doing it? There are several reasons. One of them is you think no other man can fill your heart like him. You're right—only that's the good news. See, there are all these spaces are in your heart that you should be using for the love you should be receiving. They are filled with fear instead, so you don't fully notice what you are missing. Do you really want to be a person who can never say, "Where did you go"?

The Thing

The only other thing that could be sadder is that you have this ***thing***, neatly tucked into your heart, that happened to him some time ago. This ***thing*** is what you use as an excuse to let him behave badly. You might not even know you are doing it. When he does his stuff to cause so much hurt and pain, then mysteriously you find your heart softening. It's your goodness working against you.

The thing that happened to him pops up and reminds you. You tell yourself, "He must be thinking about it again and is feeling sad." You can have these thoughts and not even realize it. You'll turn him into the victim. The only sign you might get is the fact that your heart softened after he treated you badly. Even if that were true, it doesn't give him a ticket to hurt the people who love him any time he wants. If you are repeatedly getting hurt, and repeatedly forgiving, you don't need to find out why. The only thing you need to do is to stop doing it and replace him with a model that works for you.

The fact is that every one of us on the planet has a ***thing*** that happened, including the ***man*** of your dreams and **you**. Some people have years of it. Why is it that the whole world isn't treating all their loved ones badly every time they get sad about something?

The fact is, lots of people are clinically depressed and still don't hurt the people who love them. There is something else going on with him then—the ***thing***.

What would you tell someone if they asked, "Why do you stay?" Maybe you would say something like this: "He can't help it. He needs my understanding right now."

Let's pull those words apart. It sounds like you're talking about a two-year-old who just broke something or made a mess. You need to make the best of it, and smile, and offer your help and compassion. It's those maternal instincts again. They are being used incorrectly.

Chronologically, he is not a two-year-old. He is, however, breaking things—your heart—and making a mess of your life. Only, **these items** *will be missed* and cannot be replaced.

It sounds more like you're talking about an adoption than your relationship with your partner. The sad part is, you would be talking about an adoption. You just wouldn't know it yet. The saddest part is when you finally did figure it out! Some people have gotten married and are sucked completely dry. The best years of their life are gone too, by that time.

Only a professional can explain why he behaves badly. Sometimes, not even a professional. The one thing that professionals, and women who have survived this kind of situation, agree on is that these kinds of men are cowards through and through. You will never see them giving anyone an argument that could give them a run for their money, never. That's what you're giving it all up for, a pure coward, only you don't realize it.

Sweetie, it's because you're trapped in his web of horrors. If you only listened to anyone but him for a few seconds, you could just stand up and walk away. Again, only you can save you.

I walked by a man one night, many years ago. I was laughing and talking with my girlfriends. He looked me right in the eye and said, "Gee, I wish my luck would change." I turned to him and said two words. "Make it!"

You are in charge of you. If you want your luck to change, make it change. Who else can do it? To wrap this up, he has wronged you many times over, but one of the wrongs is being made by you. You're isolated and he is not. Only you can stop that from continuing.

The first step is by only using the right words while you are discussing your situation with yourself. Never use the words he suggested. He's suggesting that his actions are out of love. He uses words like I just want us to be together and happy. All couples have problems. No relationship is perfect. Although those words make sense on one level, they don't describe your relationship with him in the slightest. Use words that describe your relationship with him. They will be fear, intimidation, sacrifices all made by one person; you. That's just a starting point.

Imagine this!

What if your parents told you that you couldn't go out with your girlfriends? What if they looked in your purse on a regular basis? Not only that, what if they didn't want you to shop or get a great job? They insisted that you not go to college. They wouldn't let you wear all the hottest styles. They threw fits if they found you on the phone. When they did take you out, what if they made your life so miserable that if you even looked around that you made sure you didn't get caught smiling at **anyone?** What if your parents wouldn't let you see your other relatives either? They even got mad if you wanted to read a romance novel or watch TV. What if their faces turned sour if you even spoke about any topic that wasn't them? They claimed it was because they loved you.

Sounds like you would be their prisoner doesn't it? In fact, if they did that, they could get in a lot of legal trouble and be made to look like horrible parents. They would be horrible parents.

Through your life they have had to stop you from doing some things you wanted to do, but not the kinds of things I just mentioned.

Of course, when you turn eighteen, you can finally do what ever you want, even with those parents. Your boyfriend doesn't agree with that. He's only just getting started. The only difference between your parents and your boyfriend is the possibility of a physical relationship. Some might say it sounds like human trafficking.

So if you really thought about it, you would be giving up every constitutional right you worked for your whole life by waiting to become an adult for the possibility of a physical relationship. Trust me those physical relationships are not hard to come by. In fact, it's more difficult to catch a cold than to get into a physical relationship. So if you do the math, you are giving up everything you will ever hold dear for something you can get easier than being sneezed on while waiting in a line.

What we are discussing is, lots of doctors have discovered that women coming off these types of relationships can not only be compared to people in concentration camps, but have found that they are just like them in every way.

So basically, you will subject yourself to the worst kind of human suffering for the possibility of a physical relationship. That is just what you are doing.

To sum it up, even prostitutes have it better than you. When they are done, they get paid and still have the freedom to come, go, and dream. I'm not saying to become a prostitute. You know that; but in these kinds of relationships you are losing, if you haven't **already** lost, the ability to come and go. You will eventually lose the ability to dream too. You can check that one out. It's easy! Just call your local battered women's shelter. I hope you do.

To me, there is nothing more frightening than losing my ability to dream, nothing! You will eventually lose yours.

Free will and relationships.

He has free will, and you don't. You're a wonderful, caring human being—most women are. You also need to be completely free to do as you please at all times. Some of the lines these textbook guys ask is, "Do you think you are just going to do anything you want?" The answer is "Yes" to that. You are trustworthy and law abiding. Doing as you please doesn't require ruining a relationship. It just means you have free will. We all have free will. It's amazing and powerful. Following your free will wherever it takes you is what makes your life unique. Free will is also a precious gift from a higher power.

Gifts are not something to just be cast aside and never used. They are now! Every time anyone gives you a gift, he **will** do more than suggest that you either not use it or actually throw it away.

Please don't give up your freedom to have a relationship. It is not part of a real relationship, since the foundation of any good relationship is trust. Remember "**trust is relying on another's integrity**"? He doesn't need your integrity. That's another precious gift you won't need.

I challenge you to explore your relationship and feelings. I'm hoping that the thought of decades together will be all the incentive you will need. Remember, nobody's perfect; but any bond formed and nurtured by trust is.

The hard truth!

This is not something that is happening **to** you. This is something that you are allowing. As long as you allow this person to control you, he will.

My father always told me, "You get what you accept." This does not mean to keep him and try not to accept his control. He cannot be fixed; do your research. I always tell my kids that two wrongs don't make a right. When they ask me what they do make I tell them, "They make two wrongs." This is going to be hard for you to hear; but here it is. These kinds of guys can actually sense if you are weak; and this allows them to take control. It doesn't mean you are weak. It could just mean you're still young and inexperienced. If you continue to let him rule your mind, heart, and world, then you are making one of those wrongs.

Someday, with a little luck and a whole lot of education, these kinds of boys will not be able to get girlfriends. For every girl who refuses to spend her time, or her whole future with this type of person, she will be part of a new reality. What I mean is, there could be a future where these kinds of boys might not even exist at all, because of you and other girls like you. You could be a link in the chain to a better world for all women everywhere. For right now, your true love is still waiting. Don't let your boyfriend make a mess out of you in the meantime. Your true love might not recognize you by time the two of you meet. Sometimes that is just what happens! I will support that claim a little more later.

Self-Esteem

Self-esteem is fragile. I have heard about cases where the woman has absolutely no self-esteem to speak of after a while with an abusive and jealous man. How does one person take something like self-esteem away from another? Well it is a complicated process.

The fact is that these kinds of men have this ability as part of their natural instincts. It seems to be part of them. They start out by saying vague things. Some of these things don't even seem harmful at all. Here are some examples:

No one could love you like me.
I'm the only one who knows what you really want.
I know what's good for you.
We are so good together.
I love you better than anyone else could.

Then the things he says start to sound a little more obvious. Here are some examples:

Where would you be if it weren't for me?
You should be thanking me for even staying with you.
No one but me wants you, not really.
I'm stupid for even wasting my time with you.
Every day I have girls coming on to me.
Do you remember what you were doing when we first met?

The breaking down of your self-esteem is a slow, tedious process. It takes time. The thing is, time is just what you are giving him every second you stay in his presence. You might only be staying with him because he is too scary to break up with. Only you can answer that. Maybe he threatens you every chance he gets? If he even gets a hint of body language that he doesn't like, he might follow through with a comment. That's when you might change your body language to make him stop. If you say something to show him you want to break up, he might follow through with a threat. That's when you might stop saying those things to make his threats stop. This is kind of like a dark waltz. These threats can be anything from physically or verbally abusing you, to threatening to hurt someone you love—or something you love instead.

I have heard it said that an average person could be brainwashed to a certain extent in just forty-eight hours. Sucking out all your self-esteem through your heart is a form of brainwashing.

How's he doing it?

One category of stealing self-esteem is accusing you of wanting to be intimate with everyone. He will suggest that you are looking at someone every chance he gets. It might get to the point where you can't even go out with your girlfriends without him thinking you want to be intimate with them too.

There will be no end to what he might accuse you of. For every time that you don't just turn around and leave, you're giving him more time to take a little more of your self-esteem.

You are secretly ashamed of letting a person treat you this way. So now you feel shame—and he is telling you it is justified. He's got you right where he wants you. Some people can be haunted their whole life by just a little bit of shame. You are getting a daily ration of it.

You might find yourself in a car with him screaming at you for looking out of the window. He will suggest that you are looking at someone. The fact that you allowed him to treat you like that and didn't leave right then cuts your self-esteem down even more. For every time you allow him to treat you in any way that is not respectful, a little more is gone.

You don't even realize it's happening. I can support my claim that it is happening. You might find yourself looking at a woman you identify with sporting a big smile on her face. You might think it is because her life is better. When you find yourself doing that, it should scream self-esteem alert. Yet it doesn't. Sporting a huge smile is one of the most natural things you can do. It is not a sign of anything but being alive. It shouldn't bring about sadness in you when you see someone else is smiling.

This might form a picture for you. What if he were to do something like that on national television? Imagine that the whole nation was watching him scream at you. He would be accusing you, in graphic detail, of your wanting to be intimate with another person.

Imagine you can't run off the stage or out of the way of the camera. You would be horribly embarrassed. The fact is, that is just how you feel whenever he does it; even when no one but you and him can hear. Not only that, you're ashamed of yourself for letting him. By staying with him you have successfully allowed him to treat you in that way. Combine that shame with his past, present, and future comments, and your self-esteem hasn't got a chance. You really can't believe you could spend the rest of your life growing as a person—or should I say thriving—under those conditions. Right?

What's in it for him?

Did you ever notice how much time that your friends and family spend begging you to break up with him? It may sound just like this:

"Please break up with him. Why would you stay with someone who does not care about you? I never see you anymore. I miss you. I care about you—he doesn't."

You know he cares about you. They don't see how he is when the two of you are alone. He is always thinking about you. You can't just take their advice when you know their advice is wrong. You're terrified of some other girl receiving all that love meant for you.

Sweetie, they are not wrong. His textbook type needs to feed on intense one-on-one interaction. You are his food! I looked up *food* for you. Here is the meaning: It's something that is needed to sustain life and promote growth. Still sound good? The one doing the consuming (that's him) is left with his life promoted. He's thriving. Remember thriving? You won't be! Once food is consumed it goes through a dramatic metamorphosis. Simply put, it is now forever changed or gone. Are (you) the food now forever changed? Some might say you are GONE! What is he feeding? He is feeding his emotional issues. He's an addict. You might think addicts need to take in a substance to be an addict, not true. You might have heard people can be addicted to behaviors. People are addicted to gambling, shopping, and gaming. Those are behaviors. That's just the short list.

He is addicted to that creepy thrill he gets from controlling his partner (you), his food. You are letting him get this thrill because you think it is something specific about his love for you making him act this way.

What does he need from (you) his food? He needs to have intense undivided attention or it's no good. How does he keep (you) his food trapped in his little web of horrors? He tricks (you) his food into thinking that all ***the good stuff*** may be right around the next corner. He ***has*** done all that; and you are convinced he sees something in you that has him bewitched! Nothing could be more sad or wrong. Well, there is one thing sadder.

Here's just one example of how he tricks (you) his food into thinking **all the good stuff** might be right around the next corner. There are some cases where girls have stayed so no other girl can ever date him. They were afraid that the minute they did the brave, smart thing, and leave to start their life with the right man, he will then be mysteriously cured. They are afraid that some other girl will receive the pleasure of his love that they suffered and waited a long time for. That's sad since no other girl will ever get the fixed version of him, because there will never be one. There's a really good reason why you're worried about that. He tricked you into worrying about it. That's just one chilling example of that dirty trick. The scary part is he only needs one, if it works. So where are (you) his food at this point?

Forever changed or GONE?

Are you forever changed or GONE? He could easily be described as a predator. A predator is something living that overtakes something else living for the sole purpose of using it as prey. Prey has only one purpose; it's food. Well, did you ever notice that just thinking about him sometimes gives you that shrinking feeling in the middle of your torso? That's the place where (you) his food lives. Did you get a cold chill? You should have! You are being consumed.

You know how some things just seem to stay with you? Well one day I found myself listening to a man give the elegy at his wife's funeral. He talked about all the things he loved about her. He said he admired how much she loved her family and her sense of style. He talked about how she made friends wherever they went. He loved how much passion she felt at the work she did. He talked about how fulfilled he felt being able to love such a wonderful woman. He said he woke every morning excited to see what she might do next. I got the feeling that the last thing he would ever do was to stop her from exploring their world. He summed it up by saying all her surprises made him a better man and he knew he could never replace her. He said that they had forty-eight years together and it wasn't nearly enough. He clearly was going to miss **sharing** his life **with** her—not sucking it **from** her. There wasn't a dry eye in the house.

Well, your partner couldn't say that stuff about the life he had with you. He doesn't want you to even see your family, have friends, or wear nice clothes. He doesn't want you to feel passionate about anything but him; if you can call being scared to death passion. He certainly couldn't watch you march off to a job you loved every day. He certainly could never stand there with his face hanging out and claim to have enjoyed sharing his life with you. Also, he won't be allowing you to make friends wherever you go.

First of all, the definition of the word *share* is a whole that is portioned off with **equal** parts allotted to more than one person. The whole is your life with him. He would have had the whole life to himself. There would end up being no portion of that life for you, nevermind an equal one. That would involve give and take. He only knows how to take; so there would be no sharing that he would be able to claim enjoying. Although, there is something he could claim that he enjoyed.

If he were being honest, which takes integrity, he would say how grateful he was that you allowed your spirit to be sucked dry all your life to satisfy his addiction. He would be able to say that in your elegy—if you died of natural causes.

It's more likely you needed an elegy because he was the one who took your life. He would then be too busy to give your elegy because he was sitting in jail. That's only if you finally had a small piece of luck and he got caught.

You would still need to have family and friends left to tell the authorities what might have happened to make you need an elegy.

By this time you would be really gone; but what would you have left behind for anyone to remember you by? You would have been so isolated that **he** would be the only one who would have recent memories of you.

That would make the loss of you all the more painful for your family and friends. That's because your family and friends would be forever changed by the fact that you are forever gone and they would have run out of chances to get you back. No one could ever fix that.

It's a poisoned life

It gets worse. Take the fact that your self-esteem has been compromised or is completely gone, combine it with the many other factors I've mentioned, and the result is a poison so deadly that only a super human could survive consuming it.

Yet, that is just what you are doing on a daily basis. I asked you before—are you super human? Eventually you *will* have to be to **break away** from this poisonous situation or even to ***stay in it***.

What is this poison? It is all the ingredients of this relationship combined. Your maternal instincts tell you he can be fixed so you stay. You are losing, or have lost, your self-esteem; so you stay. You may be hooked on your own adrenaline and or endorphins, so you stay. He treats you like a queen when he feels you slip away, so you stay. That ingredient is the starchy base that gives this poison its consistency.

He's given you cause to be too terrified to make the break, so you stay. This terror is so intense that you try to make sense of it all; by convincing yourself this relationship is doable, so you stay. The list of ingredients in this deadly concoction goes on. It's starting to require only super human strength just to resist it. Every day you stay in this relationship your self-esteem falls victim to more of this shame. The scariest thing is, it's the only thing that can save you. We have all heard the saying "*One step forward and two steps back.*" That is a person's way of saying "No progress."

When you do the math of consuming this poison, you will see the final equation: *one step back—and then two more steps back*. This is not progress. It's also a sure sign of what you are giving up to keep that relationship—everything. Relationships are supposed to add joy to your life, not poison you. The reason why you are poisoned is because you're not in a relationship. He's just another person with an addictive personality. Some of them choose gambling, shopping, or gaming. This person chooses control over another human being. The motivation is the same; that's why he seems so committed to you. HE IS! You are his gambling, shopping, or computer. You feed his addiction! Also, the last thing he wants is to train someone else. He has spent far too much time sinking his teeth into your body and soul.

Women swoon over strong men,
and he definitely has a strong hold on you!

If you think his antics are a sign of his strength just because they have a strong hold on you, they're not. They only have a strong hold on you because of your goodness. Your goodness works against you sometimes. It takes strength to be rational and reasonable. It takes strength to be considerate of the needs of others. The fact that he cannot muster up the strength to consider you or your needs on a daily basis is not strength, but the opposite; it's weakness.

You have the right to expect more than that from your partner. In fact, you should demand more than that from your partner. The whole reason we even get partners is to make our life more fulfilling. Why get a partner that makes our life less fulfilling?

The power of the English language is so amazing to me. Taking the language of an abusive partner (the same language that he uses to make it seem doable) and switching it to being said by someone who really loves you can show you how wrong it really is. All you need is the right words in the correct order to see things more clearly—then you're cured. Well, you also have to *hear* them.

Be warned; the right words to cure you will never come from his lips. He'll use his own words to try to erase every wrong he does. He usually screams the same four, "We love each other."

He's lying. It's not that you don't love each other. What's going on is you love him; and he loves him. He doesn't know how to love anyone but himself. He can't love you, ever. I can support that claim. When I do, don't feel bad. It's not a reflection on you. The good news is, your true love knows how to love. The other good news is, it's you he wants to love.

Does he love you truly?

Well, you are probably having that argument with everyone who does love you; so I thought I might take a minute to examine if he does or not. I looked up *love* in my dictionary, which I love, and here are some definitions I thought you might be interested in: Love means to have a profoundly tender and passionate affection for another. Well, you're probably thinking you are still in the game right? There's more. It also means an attraction and affection based on common interests. You do have one common interest; you both love him! It also means to show benevolence towards the one you love. *Benevolence* means to be charitable towards the **needs** of the one you love. You have needs. You're charitable towards his needs. Is he charitable towards yours?

Let's find out!

I will have no problem proving that one. You absolutely have needs. This word *needs* means something you have to have or harm will be done. You can't go the rest of your life just forgoing these needs or harm will be done to you. He has been planning just that. In fact, he will accept no less. Your needs he couldn't care less about. He is completely indifferent to them. The word *indifferent* means the opposite of love—it's not hate, like some people think.

First, I will give you the definition of the word *indifferent,* then I will list just a few of the needs which you will see he feels complete indifference to. After I am finished, you will see that he is missing the crucial piece of love—benevolence.

It's not personal.
He is not able to love you,
or anyone, the proper way.

The definition of *indifference*, which is the opposite of love, is this: it means without interest or concern. It means something that is unimportant. It means something that does not matter at all. It means showing no feeling or interest towards the needs of others. It means the lack of interest or regard towards the needs of others. In this case, the others are you and your needs. It means the inability to take a normal amount of interest in those needs due to a lack of concern or self-centeredness. Sound familiar? There's more. It means to have a cool reserve arising from a sense of superiority and/or disdain. It means he feels detached or selfish towards those needs. Those would be yours. Now that I have given you that definition, I will list the needs he is indifferent to that I am talking about.

Short list of your needs that he is indifferent to:

You need to say whatever is on your mind and get results—not pay consequences.

You need to feel safe and free of verbal and physical abuse.

You need to explore your immediate surroundings and world.

You need to buy clothes without getting the third degree.

You need to see your friends without getting the third degree.

You need to be free to talk to your friends about topics you and your friends choose.

You need to shop without explaining afterwards.

You need to leave the house on a regular basis without explaining.

You need to visit family and friends in the spur of the moment.

You need to continue to get an education if you so choose.

You need to pursue your own interests and/or career.

You need to be able to work where you choose.

You need to start new projects, just because.

You need to be free to change your mind, just because.

You need to be passionate about everything without explaining it has nothing to do with sex or the desire to be unfaithful.

You need to be free to apply make-up and wear any hairstyle you choose.

You need to be with child without promising to have a paternity test after.

You need to change the way you look just because the feeling struck you.

You need to look out the passenger side window of a car without getting the third degree.

You need to have privacy with your body and personal effects.

You need to have male friends if you want. It doesn't mean you want them as a partner.

You need to be free to love, love, love what you might love.

Yes, that is just the short list. The actual list would be too long to add here. It's also unnecessary because you are a smart person, so I don't need to list everything.

You can see where I am going with your needs, which he is completely indifferent to. These are not just needs, but also rights. In order to lose these needs and/or rights, you have to commit a felony. Even then only the authorities can take them away—not ever your partner. You are giving them up freely to prevent your partner from becoming inflamed with anger.

If you try to live your life without these needs you will be harmed in some obvious way. One of these ways is you won't thrive—remember, to flourish and grow vigorously.

He is completely indifferent to these needs. Don't forget that indifference is the opposite of love. You can't have love without benevolence because you will always have needs. There is no love if there is no benevolence.

Without benevolence
there is no true love!

Here is the way your partner should feel about the complete list of your needs: He should be generous and giving. He should make sure your needs are met in ample proportions. He should always be making sure that your needs are not slipping away in order to have his needs met instead. He should get pure pleasure from being the reason your needs **are** being met.

We know you're doing that, but is he? He is not! He doesn't love you and never will; because he can't. He's not your true love. Your true love knows how to do all that and much more. He won't need years of professional help to teach him either. Of course, we already know that eighty-five percent of the time it doesn't work anyway. I was told, off the record, that the fifteen percent success rate does not actually exist because they go back to their old ways without reporting it to the program they were working with.

How and why he's making it happen.

In the first place, any person who is jealous and controlling is incapable of caring about your needs. It is a fundamental component of this emotional issue.

How is he getting away with being indifferent to your needs? First, he is actually ***using*** the word ***love*** to pull it off. He's telling you that he loves you so much he just can't take the chance that your needs being met might result in his losing you.

That's backwards, plain and simple—and you're falling for it. In fact, you are falling for it hook, line, and sinker. One of many of the reasons you're falling for it is because he's not saying it like that.

He seems totally committed to you. He's really obsessed with holding your physical body hostage while he sucks your spirit dry. It seems on the surface that he is really into you, the you deep inside, but it's not that at all. He freaks out every time your spirit wants to soar, so he cannot be into that you. So why can't you hear what he **is** saying? That's still what he's saying. He is using language like a craftsman would use any tool. Also, he gets snippy and condescending while he repeats your words; the ones you use when you want to do something that doesn't involve him. This is designed to keep you just a little off. That's because for the most part it works. They all do it. It's as if they all go to the same convention for jealous and controlling partners. Even the doctors who treat these men don't understand how they work inside. Doctors sometimes claim fear is at the root of this addiction. They claim he is afraid of something that even he doesn't know about. The only thing they do know is that their nature is to be completely selfish and self-absorbed.

We've all known fear. We all don't go around tearing up the personal lives of everyone who lets us in. Another way he makes it happen is he's charming—just enough to string you along from screw up to screw. He has to be; or he would be out of business. Then he might just skip charming and get right to frightening.

Even though these tactics seem opposite, they can be used simultaneously or just one at a time. They are the framework of a device called control. It works well. It has to. He has plans to control every part of you, inside and out, until you are nothing but a sack of flesh willing to give in to his every whim just to keep him quiet. How close are you to that right now?

Respect

Does he respect you? I can answer that. ***No***! Respect means ***to refrain from intruding upon***—BLANK! The "blank" is anything and everything that is important to you.

Let's check the list of things important to you that he intrudes upon:

Self-esteem
Confidence
Friendships with others
Sense of style
Sense of well-being
Any and every freedom
Your dignity

That is the micro list—you live the whole list. He does not respect you. He doesn't. I'm talking about the you that lives in the middle of your torso. This is the place where you live, where you feel, where you dream of soaring. He does not refrain from intruding upon anything that is important to you. He never will; because he can't. He does not love you or respect you. He does, however, need you desperately.

You can feel that desperation coming from him. Of course you can. You can feel it, and you think it means he loves you. Sadly, that is all you are getting from him. Actions speak louder than words; you've heard that! His words tell you that he recognizes your need for respect; his actions tell you he's a liar. As I mentioned before, he's an addict. He's desperate to stay with you to feed his **vice**. A vice is a **personal shortcoming or foible**. A *foible* is a **weakness or failing of character**.

If he does not have you, or someone like you, in his life he cannot thrive. He cannot feed his vice. If you are the person in his life feeding this vice, ***you cannot thrive***. It's you or him.

Only one of you will thrive. It's that simple. In a normal relationship both people thrive. That's because both people give respect and both people take respect. In a normal relationship there's enough respect for two.

Don't say "I do"!

What would happen if you did marry him? I can tell you exactly what would happen.

First, I'd like to tell you why you would say yes. It's because you'd be thinking it would put his fears of losing you to bed once and for all. He'd tell you that himself too.

You couldn't be more wrong. It's those darn maternal instincts again. Not only would he not simmer down—he would actually escalate his terrorizing. That's right! That's because now he would **own you!** It would get worse and worse, because you were—and he would scream this—"HIS WIFE"! He would be "in the right"!

Whenever a person like him feels he is in **the right** he moves into high gear. It usually starts within forty-eight hours after saying "I do." Your life would become even more of a living hell. It would never end.

Find out from your local women's center what happens after the boyfriend turns into the husband. Find out everything you can. If you are a religious person, then you could believe that once you are married, you have to stay married. Don't jump from the pan to the fire. It's hot in the fire! Get out of the pan. Get off the stove altogether.

Don't blame your intelligence.

It's not because you are not intelligent. You are! Don't think that this isn't happening to intelligent women all over the world. It is. All women are at risk at certain times in their lives. Please know that men suffering from this type of addiction live in all tax brackets. Plus it's part of your nature as a good and giving person to give him a break. You just haven't been doing the math to see how many breaks that has added up to.

He will use beautiful words to convince you that all his actions toward your needs are because he loves you. You truly want to believe him. If his words and actions don't correspond then his words must be meaningless. His actions take precedence over his words when they don't match; they always will. There is no other conclusion to draw.

The only thing that should hold any merit is his actions. His actions will tell you implicitly that he does not feel benevolence towards your needs and thus cannot possibly love you. Don't take it personally. He can't ever love you the right way. He can't truly love anyone the right way. Only the right man can do that. That's where you should be putting your ***precious time*** and ***energy***.

Is it worth taking the time to tell him?

I could add a to-die-for speech here to rattle off to your partner on needs, love, and benevolence and how you can't have one without the other; but it wouldn't be worth the paper it was written on. It's not because it wouldn't be a great speech. It's because it will fall on deaf ears. The only person who would be moved by this speech would be a partner who doesn't need to hear it in the first place. That person wouldn't need to hear it because he knows it in every cell of his being already. He has known it all his life.

I would like to mention that in your partnership there are two people; you and your partner. Your partner should love you and you should love you too. If you are allowing your partner to be indifferent towards your needs, then you are also being indifferent towards your needs. You are in charge of your needs. Take charge!

New facts need new choices.

Once you know the facts, it's then time to make the hard choices; but it's always going to be up to you. This may seem irrelevant—but it's not. How many times have you heard people put down famous people for being in shape? They still have to be alone with food; unless they have agreed to be sealed in a cave most of the day. They are in shape because they are committed to helping themselves. Without that commitment there would be no results. Short of your family and friends kidnapping you today, you are the only one who can save you. Making those fact-based choices as soon as possible will result in your needs being back on the table as soon as possible. That's not just a fact, it's also a promise!

If you are considering killing some time with him, hoping he might just work his problems out, and thinking you are only hurting yourself; think again. As long as you have family and friends WHO *do* love you, there is no such thing as only hurting yourself. I can't remind you of that often enough. Think about this—only about fifteen percent of these kinds of men can find help in therapy and even then only slightly. That's not very many.

In case you never liked math—for every hundred guys with this problem who try to get help, eighty-five don't get fixed. Those are your odds; if he even tries to seek help. He won't look for help until he has wrecked many years of your life. So to spell it out; he will have to wreck many of your years, be big enough to seek help, and still have an eighty-five percent chance of not getting any results. Meanwhile, your true love is still waiting to meet you—or enjoying his life with someone else. Like I said, that fifteen percent isn't even accurate. They typically go back to their old ways without reporting to the program they worked with.

Don't stay in too long!

I know it sounds a little unbelievable; but I have personally witnessed a mother say that she didn't recognize her own daughter who was in this kind of relationship.

Her daughter's face was so contorted from fear and stress that she didn't know her for the first few seconds when she finally saw her in the emergency room of their local hospital.

She wasn't bleeding or battered on her face; it was her expressions that were commonplace by this time.

If your true love doesn't recognize you because you stayed too long or went back too many times you could lose him too. Having the courage to go through the adjustment period is the most important and hardest step. The definition of *courage* is being afraid and doing it anyway. Then the courage will come; as well as the rewards of that particular act of courage. The good news is, your true love does not need treatment. He just needs you to be single and recognizable when he finally meets you.

If you stay with this man too long you'll change inside so much that it will change the way you look. Your true love knows what you look like, even though he might not have met you yet. Take that away and you might never hook up with your true love.

In case of emergency, break glass!

Okay, that takes care of a lot of very powerful reasons that you have not left him yet. They are emotional—you feel intense fear and love. And physical; you're hooked on your own adrenaline and/or endorphins. That's huge. It is really understandable why you feel so glued to him. You will need to use all your smarts and strength here to see your situation.

You might actually love him. That makes it more difficult. Just expect it to be hard. The payoff to fix this is well worth it. I promise on everything good. When you go to him and begin the break up there are several classic things that will happen.

I will breeze over them in the order that they will happen. This order is based on research and the memories of several friends. The first thing that will happen is he will think it is a false alarm. He will spin a wonderful web of words that could make any woman's inner self turn to overcooked spaghetti. He will be an absolute craftsman here. He will use phrases like, "I promise to try harder. I love you so much." He will remind you of popular love songs that the two of you have listened to together. He might even play one while he looks into your eyes. When that doesn't seem to work he will switch to pretty sentences with words like marriage, children, homes, and growing old together in them.

Then, when you stick to your guns, the next step is he will get angry and accuse you of doing something terrible to him and the relationship. This can start by his accusing you of cheating. Then it can get ugly. It can and will be the most danger you will ever be in.

You should set up your conversation in your home with other family members in other rooms. When he starts getting angry, and he will, you might still feel safe. But, work with me here, leave the room quickly and send someone in to ask him to leave. After that it gets fuzzy. He may start crying. That's just to knock you off your stand.

When he starts crying and carrying on, it will take super human strength to finish the job. You'll have to muster up some. This is all part of his crafty little web of horrors. Even after he leaves, he will still be on the crying part. He will try to call or track you down everywhere. Don't let him catch you alone for a long time. A long time could mean forever. It varies from addict to addict. This is critical to your success. This is not a step you can skip. If you make it through these critical phases, hang on. The next few months are going to be hard. You WILL feel lost being off the physical and emotional roller coaster he has had you on. After that passes, and it will, you will be free. You might still be a little bit of a mess. Some final healing might be required. Everyone's situation is unique. If you fail and stay together, he will trust you even less after that.

You don't need me to tell you how that will change your life. You will get the full treatment in person; but you get the picture. If you need help, please ask someone. There is no shame in needing help, ever. There is only shame in not asking.

Adjustment Period

If you do manage to get away from this man, there will be an adjustment period. Not expecting this period will be the greatest threat to your success. Of course, even something undesirable that has lasted any length of time requires an adjustment period.

Let's face it—it wasn't all undesirable right? There were glimmers. I was sad when I got my braces off. I hated them, yet still I missed them. It passed. When you expect it, and know how it might feel, it might make it easier to deal with. I can tell you how it might feel. It might feel like you lost something really important. You will feel lonely. You might just simply feel little lost. The quiet times you'll have, immediately following the break, will seem more like the end of the world than peaceful. It is peaceful. You just don't recognize it. You will again. You will start to convince yourself that he is just misunderstood. You will start to wonder if he is seeing anyone, if he might be treating them better than you. You will think that leaving has taught him the valuable lesson he needed and now it is safe to come back.

That is the most dangerous feeling of all. The other feeling that equals that one is the longing for those highs and lows. Yes, you will long for that. It's something I can't really explain. It can probably be compared to any addictive drug—even though it's one your own body makes.

In case you forgot, it's adrenaline and/or endorphins. You're a junkie. I promised I'd explain, so here it is. You have spent so much of your time expending energy of all kinds. You get high on one energy and low on another. His moods do that to you. When you leave him you'll have periods every day when you'll pace back and forth like a caged animal. It can happen right around the typical times you might normally be interacting with him; it can happen anytime. It's your body coming down cold turkey from those highs and lows. You might feel like a runner who is trapped in a house and can't run. Those physical feelings can translate to emotional ones. It will feel like you miss him; but what you miss are those chemicals.

The good news is, it passes. This might sound silly; but when it's happening you might try sit-ups, jumping-jacks, push-ups and things like that. This is just to use up all that energy you would have used staying with him. How many you might have to do depends on how vigorous your relationship was.

He's no help either. He calls and tells you he knows what's best for you. How could he? You don't even have that answer.

You wonder, "What if he is right?" He begs you to let him prove it. You don't have to know what's best for you yet. Say no to that. You only have to know what is not best for you.

It is not best to be his emotional hostage for life. In fact, it's just one of those creepy instances where they all seem to go to the same convention for controlling men. They all say that! He's not unique. Your true love is.

As the days wear on you will become even more curious about his where-a-bouts and what he might be doing. It is just like coming off any addictive drug. You need time to regain the correct way to see the world. Please remember that these men are in it for life.

We have all heard that some people go through treatment and recover; but even the treatment centers for these kinds of men claim close to eighty-five percent failure. Imagine; eighty-five percent don't get better. I can't remind you of that enough times. Once again—just to drive it home—that fifteen percent success rate is likely inaccurate. In actuality, those supposed success stories will probably return to their old ways but will never check in with their providers again.

You'll have to deal with the feeling of being alone during the adjustment period. You'll have to do it while he is still hanging on. What do I mean by feeling alone while he is hanging on?

You're finally free—or are you?

I hate to bring this up; but it's a must. There's still one more problem; **stalking.** Even though you're in the home stretch of getting yourself free, you're actually facing the hardest part. The chance of his not stalking you for a period of time after you break up is slim.

Yes, it's more than a possibility; it's a definite probability. It's also likely going to go on for quite a while. It seems the longer you stay in this kind of situation, the longer the stalking continues. There is no telling how long it will last. That's one thing no one can tell you—we all find out together.

What is stalking? Well you might already know, but I'll tell you anyway. *Stalking* is when he comes to your house and you (or preferably someone else) make him leave; then he comes back. It happens so many times per day you have adopted a new habit of looking out the window. This habit becomes something you do instead of living your life. Also, when he is not sitting out in front of your house—or even while he is—he is calling and calling and calling. This happens until the sound of your phone ringing makes you crazy. You'll eventually have to turn the ringer off. Of course, you'll then feel out of touch with the world. That's what he wants. Block him. Get a new cell and just use that for a while. Let his calls go to voicemail. He follows you around in your car so much that you can't stop looking in the rear-view mirror to see if he is there. This newly adopted behavior is just as dangerous as any other known distraction. Be careful. He will come to your school, work, or friends' houses looking for you. He stands outside making a scene. He claims he only wants to talk. He doesn't! What he does want is to intimidate you with so much pressure that you agree to start up the relationship again. He will proclaim that he knows what he did was wrong and it will never happen again. He tells you that your leaving him has taught him the valuable lesson he needed. It's more graphic in person. At any rate, when you hang on to your "No," he'll start screaming that this proves he was right about you all along. Don't fall for that intimidation.

It's the oldest and dirtiest trick in the book. It's the oldest because it works so well. It's the dirtiest because it works so well. He is now well-versed with all your guilt-buttons. He pushes them mercilessly. He has forced you to become his personal trained seal. He takes great pleasure in watching you succumb to that.

There are laws against this. Make no mistake, this is a crime. It's called stalking. What it really is, is extortion. It's the crime of using force, intimation, or abuse of authority to obtain an ultimate goal. The authority he has over you is the deep fear he has fabricated within you over the course of your relationship. Let's face it; it is also the fact that he is bigger and stronger than you. If that's not authority, I don't know what is. For some reason, they decided to simply call it stalking, even though it fits the criteria of extortion exactly. See, sometimes people get beat up in extortion; but it's more complicated than just battery. That's why they couldn't only call it battery. Likewise, stalking is more complicated than simply following someone. He abuses, forces, and intimidates for the purpose of his ultimate goal. He uses his authority to achieve it too.

The crime of extortion is a felony of the first offense. For stalking it only becomes a felony after the second offense. This could add up to many years of suffering at his hands. The more you know about the laws, the more they can work for you. Put up with nothing! Press charges immediately! Make them stick! Maybe he won't want to be a felon and stop. Maybe someday the courts will see stalking as heinous a crime; as it really is. If you fall victim to his act, you yourself could serve a life sentence. Don't let it happen. You owe him nothing; but he owes you your life back.

In order to press stalking charges you have to have documentation. You will need as much proof as possible. It would be great if you had the money to hire a detective to help you collect documentation. Without documentation you can't make these charges stick. If you don't, then it's up to you. Keep any messages he sends you. Have your friends collect anything relevant they can find. Be ready with a camera wherever you go. That way, you can show where you were and how many times your paths crossed. This is one of the sticking points of stalking. Public places can be used as just coincidences. We both know that they won't be—but if you have proof of how many times it's happened, it will be hard for him to call them coincidences. If you get a restraining order then you can have him arrested if he comes too physically close to you. Make sure you use the police to your advantage as much as possible. That way, they can corroborate your claims and make the other evidence you collected on your own look more credible. Don't ever change your mind and not press charges. He will be working like the dickens to make you change your mind. Don't fall for it! You can only delay the inevitable and make yourself look like the Boy Who Cried Wolf. The police hate that. You want them on your side. If they see a person who is serious they will treat you like one; then you can get matching results. There is nothing more stylish than success.

Rules engraved in stone for surviving this part

Stalking is not the ultimate compliment—as you will soon find out. A compliment makes you feel good. You will feel terrified and trapped once again. You should start by finding out what are the stalking laws in your area. Also, keep your phone charged at all times. Keep it hidden near your bed at night. I say hidden so if he breaks in, he doesn't find it before you do. You also need pepper spray. You don't need to take him down; just get away. You need to take classes that teach you simple techniques to help you get away from a person holding you physically hostage. You need a restraining order; this is supposed to keep you safe. Only rely on it to put a crimp in his schedule by having him put in jail every time he violates it.

There is no telling how long it will go on. There is one thing I can tell you. When he calls, if you make the mistake of answering, you must hang up without a word. It might be wiser not to answer the phone at all. Let his call go to voicemail. If your voice is on the recording, change your message to the default. Don't even let him hear your voice in that small way. Get an unlisted number if need be.

When he sees you out in public, run without a word. The slightest syllable from you can and will be blown up into a declaration of love from you to him. This is no joke. It's as true as it is ridiculous. Do not give him a look in the eye or a word. Just cut the cord and don't look back. This is the only way to shorten the stalking. I don't know of any ways to end the stalking. You need to get the latest information from women's centers in your area. If you underestimate this problem you could end up dead. You'll leave the people who do love you grieving for you for the rest of their lives. You don't want that. If you remember the good times, and give him even a minute, you'll let your goodness get you into a big mess you might never get out of. **Resist!**

Meanwhile, he's remembering things that never happened. He's remembering that you cheated and ruined the relationship all by yourself. I guarantee you, the things going on in his mind are miles and miles from you and your normal thoughts. These kinds of men don't like to be dumped. In fact, you couldn't do anything worse to him.

The things he is capable of doing to you once you convince him it's over are inconceivable. Of course, I'm forced to mention that if you find yourself in the unenviable position of having a child with him, it then becomes murky water. The object of saving yourself from harm still remains the same; but instead of removing yourself from his world you will have to instead train him to see the world without you as his partner. Use a mediator to transfer messages, and use a mediator to transfer the child back and forth for visits. This is, of course, if your child will be safe while visiting. Only you know when that will be possible. One sign is when he stops using every trick in the book to see you. Be warned; when these kinds of men suddenly seem calm, that is sometimes when they are the most dangerous. Use your instincts. They will be your main saving grace. Don't let the fact that you have his child make you do anything different. You have to stay safe; that has to be your main objective. If you could get a child to adequately answer the question of what would his or her main objective **be,** it would be "To keep my mommy safe." Of course, your objective is to keep your child safe too. You need to go through the court system to do this right. It's all still doable. Ask for help and advice from professionals in your area. Put him out of the business of hurting you.

If you ever find yourself in this situation and you are living alone—and he knows where you live—move. I don't care how much you love your place. Once the stalking starts you cannot live alone. You can pick up your life again when and if it stops. Don't try to be the movie of the week, hero woman. Just do the safest, smartest thing, and move! If you don't want to **keep** moving, move in with someone you trust.

Final threat to your success!

In short, you are the final threat to your success. Are you wondering how you might be feeling about the break up right about now? You might hear people say, "Now do you see what kind of a person he is?"

In my opinion, even if you do finally see it you could still be feeling any number of ways. They would all be perfectly normal. Even if you were still feeling sad and lost it would make sense.

It's literally like surgery to get your heart back—even if you're the one who wants it. This is as hard as life gets! The fact that you do not understand what you are feeling is the threat. If you could take your feelings and put them under a microscope and examine them you would be well-served. You can't do that. You have to use your instincts—or you can use the experiences of other women from the past. We can only talk about other women from the past who have been through this. Only you can use your instincts.

There are women from the past that thought these feelings meant that they made a mistake and they went back. Some of them realized their mistake quite quickly and had to start again from square one—which is the dramatic escape. Some of these women didn't realize quite so quickly and lost their lives while sitting at the dinner table with him (or showering, or even sleeping). There are so many ways they lost their lives. We don't need to examine them all—they are all tragic. That's the main thing to know. Then there were women from the past who realized they were simply inundated with too many feelings and bravely stuck with the main objective. They won the final battle and the war. You're fighting tooth and nail to rid yourself of this man. He is causing you fear, anger, sadness, and many more intense feelings. It causes a cloud to follow you around.

Let's face it; dreams we have for love die hard. It doesn't matter that you proved, beyond a reasonable doubt, that the relationship is toxic and unhealthy. How do you think any woman would feel listening to a man scream, "You made a mistake, take me back"? It's called wearing you down. Why it works is one of the mysteries of the heart. Until your heart stops messing things up, stuff it in the trunk. Let your brain drive! You are in the middle of the second adjustment period. You would never have had to go through a second one—without the stalking.

You might find yourself wondering if you are having second thoughts about breaking up or if this is the normal way to feel. It's normal—so stop worrying. Don't focus on the what-ifs! You can't rewrite history; even history that just happened. What I mean is, you can't gather all the good times and turn them into the only things you remember. The power we derive from history is the learning. Another thing you might be experiencing is physical exhaustion. In fact, if you weren't physically exhausted, it would be a miracle. It will all pass. Hang on, you're almost home. Don't let this last difficult step wear on your resolve. Remember the super human strength I mentioned several times? This is one of the many times you will need it.

Don't let any of those sad feelings stop you from your main objective. There are many ways to muster super human strength. I'd like to mention some. One way to summon this kind of strength is to keep your eyes on the prize. The prize is your true love and your life. It's all your dreams coming true. It's freedom to experience your world without someone terrifying you back into the dark.

Also, you need to get your self-esteem and confidence back. You might be wondering if you ever had any self-esteem and confidence in the first place. Locating one's self-esteem and confidence often seems like trying to catch an invisible butterfly. Can you imagine how hard an invisible butterfly would be to catch? They are hard enough to catch when you can see them. Like self-esteem, you might not even know if it was there at all. Don't worry, there are easy ways to fix that. Without ever having any self-esteem or confidence to speak of, you can get it by doing these five things. I've found that they work well.

The first is to stop running the reels in your mind. What I mean is, all those bad things that happened to you; not just with your boyfriend.

I mean anything that happened that seems to haunt you. When these memories come flooding into your head, stop them. I don't care if you have to think about puppies and doorknobs. Just do it. Once the bad thought is successfully gone, you can go back to what you were thinking about before you got rudely interrupted by them. They do tend to come out of nowhere.

Every time you stop the reel, you don't get weaker. Every time you don't get weaker, you get more comfortable with this exercise. Every time you stop the reel from running in your head, you get better at it. You also see the purpose of the whole thing. The purpose is to keep your thoughts in the happy or productive so you don't have fragments or whole days ruined. You can control your thoughts. Don't worry about forgetting to do it once and a while. What I mean is you might find that you forgot to do this exercise so many times you feel right back where you started. You won't be right back where you started. The only way to fail is by giving up. Until the second that you give up comes, you haven't failed. When you forget for a time, just start over. This will be a valuable skill for your whole life.

You might have a habit of **not** looking people in the eye and not even know it. So the second is, always look people in the eye. I don't mean if it puts you in harm's way like when you are around any kind of violent people; I mean in your ordinary **life.** Don't stare penetratingly. Just look them in the eye casually. Look like you own the place and you belong there. You can look away from time to time while you are in thought, or you can watch other people with great confidence. See how many times they look away for how long and for what reasons. It's very important to do this when you talk to people and while just walking through life. You will notice, when you start to do this, you have to hold your head up in order to do it in the first place. Just the act of holding your head up alone builds self-esteem and confidence. People around you will feel you are proud and confident and soon so will you. They will look at you differently while you are doing that, and treat you differently too. Watch. You'll see what I mean. You'll like it too. This will be a valuable skill your whole life.

The third is, you should always nurture your opinions. See the thing is, you don't know what you are passionate about unless you do. You **have** to say what's on your mind out loud and talk about it as much as possible—without driving everyone away of course. That way you know what you love and what you only like. When you are too afraid to say them out loud, they slip away and you never get to know **you.** When you have an opinion about anything you should express it. Some of them will fade away and some of them will take on a life of their own. None of that can happen while you are only thinking them. Knowing what you feel passionate about builds self-esteem and confidence that won't let you down. This will be a valuable skill your whole life.

The fourth is, help people whenever possible. Again, I don't mean put yourself in harm's way. I don't mean to make yourself late for appointments either. I mean small things; until you are ready for larger things. It helps you to see that you are just as important as everyone else. When you do these kinds of things, people will thank you. There is so much value in being thanked; it boggles the mind.

It brings self-esteem and confidence directly to you. It's as if the self-esteem fairy sprinkles you with more each time. You can feel it too. Soon your soul will swell with pride by the smallest act. It sounds silly, but that's just what happens. There are so many variables in this one. You just have to get out there. Live your life and they will find you. This will be a valuable skill your whole life.

The fifth one is my favorite. If you ever need help, ask someone you trust for help, and let him or her help you. It's okay! Asking for help when you need it creates self-esteem and confidence too. This will be a valuable skill your whole life.

What if your future partner was a position that you had available at your very own business for applicants to apply for?

You would only have one position available, right? The fact is, that actually is your situation. May I suggest a long, intense interviewing process? This means many questions over many dates. At some time, there should also be a trial period. Just like the kind you would expect during the first few months at your new job. After that, if your trial period proves that you don't have your true love working for you, it's a whole lot easier to look for the next candidate for the job if there were no promises or benefits given during this time. How many ads for jobs read, "Looking for the first horrible person that comes along"? You do need, want, and must have the best person for the job, right? ABSOLUTELY!

The bottom line.

He has been very busy telling you that you can't do better than him. Don't believe him.

You can! Even if you had a third eye in the middle of your forehead you could do better than him. That's a fact. I can support that statement.

He will abuse you forever. That's because he will always be a jealous control freak. If you think his jealousy is a sign of his love, think again. It's actually a sign of a deep routed emotional problem. It's easy to put a romantic spin on jealousy; but that's part of the problem. There's really nothing romantic about jealousy. Again, I turned to my beloved dictionary for you. *Jealousy* means to be **resentful** and to **not want** someone to be **successful.** Here's an example. When you like someone's hair or clothes, you envy them. You might wish you could enjoy hair and clothes like that, but you still want **them** to have **their** hair or clothes. On the other hand, if you were jealous of their hair and clothes, you would be doing everything in your power to separate them from their hair and clothes. Who hasn't heard stories of that nature? See the difference between jealousy and envy? He's not just envious of your other relationships. If he were only envious, you **could** put a romantic spin on **that!** He doesn't want you to **have** a relationship with him and relationships with anyone else. He's going to do everything possible to **separate** you from your other relationships and your needs.

He will never allow you to be successful in enjoying anyone else's company, ever. You were looking for **love** and found only **jealousy instead**. They don't call jealousy the green eyed monster for nothing.

Your relationship with your partner is the only thing you have in your life that's all about you. Your parents have each other, and maybe other children. Your siblings have your parents and their own lives. Your children will eventually grow up and have their own lives. Your friends go back and forth from their lives to spend time with you. Your partner is the only person in your life that is all about you and your needs, and vice versa. A relationship without your needs being met in ample proportion has no YOU in the equation. Without YOU, there is no relationship that is all about YOU. With him as your partner, you failed completely at finding that all about YOU intimate relationship! I proved, beyond a reasonable doubt, that without your needs being important to **him,** what he's feeling cannot be love.

Do you really think that the best you can do is to fail completely? Do you? Let's go over all the hot points so far. He doesn't love or respect you and never will. He doesn't trust you and never will. He doesn't want you to be successful in anything at all—***except*** being of service to him and never will. He doesn't have faith in you and never will. He hasn't been finished being raised and never will. You want to have your free will and this relationship, but you never will. You want him to stop isolating you, but he never will. You want him to be the kind of person you can love and tolerate forever, but he never will. You desperately want him to stop breaking your heart, but he never will.

So by the time you're the next woman being rushed off somewhere on the 11 o'clock news (maybe to jail, or the hospital, or even the morgue), you will have given up everything you've ever had except him. Drained? Stop this madness right now and you'll definitely recover. ***Later on,*** there is a good chance that you never will.

He says that you can't do better than him and his love. You ***were*** looking for love, but found an emotional issue with jealousy as the main symptom instead. You might in fact love him. So he did find love in you. You, on the other hand, failed completely. You didn't find love at all. He says that's the best you can do—is to be a complete failure. When you think about it, using a simple dictionary makes everything so clear. Really think about this statement: IF HE **IS** THE BEST YOU CAN DO, FAILING COMPLETELY **IS** THEN THE BEST YOU CAN DO.

I'm giving you two homework assignments at this point. Everything you need to know to do it is in what you just read. If you could sum up his contribution to this relationship in a verbal equation it would sound like this:

Here's the first one. If you love it—and it's not him—he doesn't want you to have it. Show him something and tell him you love it. Make up a story that doesn't involve another partner. Maybe you could tell him you bought it yourself. Make sure it is something you really don't like at all. That's because he will then become very busy planning to remove it from your life. In the next argument he will make it the focal point. Maybe he will hold it up in a threatening manner. It may or may not be gone during that first argument. I do predict, however, that you won't have it for long after you reveal how much you love it. He might break it, or he could just demand that you get rid of it. I know it sounds silly. Do it anyway.

That's it. Pay close attention to his words and actions. Soon you will see the equation as if it were screaming at you. When you see the equation you should be cured. I promise. Human nature dictates that sometimes, in order for information to really become a part of you, it needs to be repeated. Feel free to read this through again and again; it may be the reason you don't *live* it again and again.

I have added some blank lined pages at the end of this book for your second homework assignment. Write a detailed description of your perfect man.

Be brutally honest with his good side. In other words, add, add, and add the good stuff. I think you will find that this man does exist. If you can dream him up, he lives and breathes. You just have not found him yet. He is worth waiting for; I promise. Also, write in red ink to quickly find the paragraphs you want; in order to detail some of the tantrums your jealous, controlling partner is having. You'll see the differences in your dream man and the one you have now.

Remember, you could live to be in your hundreds and still be healthy these days. With those kinds of years ahead, shouldn't you make every effort to spend them as happily as possible? Important things need to be repeated more than once. Here goes another one. As long as *you* have other people who do love you there is no such thing as only hurting yourself. ***There just isn't!*** Staying with him, in the hopes he will change, hurts you. It hurts all the people who do love you—because they love you.

While you're with him, he's responsible for hurting you, and you're responsible for hurting the people who do love you.

Sink or Swim

Bound by Freedom

I am free to love my friends and family,
and am only entangled
by worry of losing thee

I am free to go, yet choose to stay
because I can change my mind day by day

I am free to be faithful out of love, not fear
Lovers bound together freely forge a bond no
human can tear

Because I am truly free
serendipity's the only unexpected strike on me.

Freedom's a privilege I take for granted,
I could never do that if it were slanted

I am free with mind and body and spirit
to imagine possibilities infinite
I exploit those I see true
and leave the rest to save integrity and you

All who live happily within the flow
of life's natural restrictions
enjoy the sweetest of life's convictions

Notes

Notes

Notes

Notes

Notes

Notes

Notes

Notes

Notes

Notes

Notes

Notes

Notes

Notes

Notes

Notes

Notes

Notes

Notes

Notes

Notes

CPSIA information can be obtained
at www.ICGtesting.com
Printed in the USA
LVHW022114260122
709317LV00008B/102

9 781955 123594